Table of Contents

Introduction:	2
The matter of expressing oneself:	4
What is posted online remains accessible indefinitely:	5
You are not (in)visible:	7
Context, tone, and audience:	9
The workplace in the era of technology:	12
You've been tagged:	14
Potential repercussions of a social media mistake:	15
It's over:	16
Managing social media platforms:	17
The Streisand effect:	18
How to stay out of trouble:	19

Introduction:

This book is not going to tell you to throw social media out the window. This book is not going to tell you to never post again on any of your social media pages, and this book is also not going to teach you how to be a masterful social media influencer. Instead, this book will aim to tell you exactly how to have fun online, without jeopardising your job, your safety or losing your reputation.

Now while many books concentrate only on online safety and cyber and digital marketing - very few books actually tell us how easy it is to damage and do harm to the reputation of your company or you personally.

This book is pretty straightforward, no footnotes, long legal acts or boring case studies. Simply put, this book will be an easy to read and understand social media guideline that you can read to either guide yourself, or your employees through the uncharted waters of the digital age.

Digital content is dangerous content

Just like your email, your social media can create business records or electronically stored information (ESI). Any employee that uses a company computer to tweet on Twitter, network of Facebook, or upload a video on YouTube, content created on a company computer or network may be subpoenaed, and these records can be used as evidence in lawsuits and regulatory investigations.

What does this mean to you as an employee? This means that your social media posts, either posted while at work or at home, but on your work, computer essentially belong to your company and can be used by them in any court case or in any investigations. Be careful where you post from. This seems a small and insignificant detail in the vast world of social media, but this is an important detail to note especially if you are using your work phone or laptop for personal texts, social media, and internet browsing.

A further note to add is that even if you are posting or browsing on a personal device if the content you are engaging in is harmful in any way to your employer, and or company of employment this may be enough grounds for suspension and or removal from your position.

Now, this all sounds very scary - but think about this for a moment, you are an employer. Your employee is for example engaging in online stalking of children and it becomes an investigation against him/her. This would be enough grounds for a suspension of his/her work duties and position as social media might have been the starting point, but the criminal aspect has encompassing repercussions for this individual. This might be a harsh example, but even a simple act of subtle racism or sexism can have such consequences and it is important to note that many jokes shared, have an undertone of such context.

The matter of expressing oneself:

Mike Meecham thought freedom of speech means you can post a phrase like "Sieg Heil" on YouTube. That is simply not true.

In 2019, Mark Meechan, a Scottish YouTuber, was found guilty of a hate crime for posting a video on his channel that showed him training his girlfriend's dog to perform a Nazi salute in response to the phrase "Sieg Heil" and other anti-Semitic phrases.

Meechan claimed that the video was intended as a joke and a commentary on the absurdity of the modern political climate, but he was charged with violating the Communications Act of 2003, which prohibits "grossly offensive" messages. Meechan was fined £800 and sentenced to community service, sparking a debate about free speech and the appropriate limits of online expression. Some argued that Meechan's video was protected by the right to freedom of expression, while others maintained that hate speech should not be tolerated in any form.

The case of Mike Meecham raises important questions about the limits of freedom of speech. While it is important to protect freedom of expression and the right to express one's views, this must be balanced against the need to protect individuals and groups from harm. In the case of hate speech, there is a fine line between free speech and speech that incites violence, hatred, or discrimination. Many argue that hate speech should not be protected under the banner of free speech, as it can cause real harm to individuals and communities.

The Meecham case also highlights the challenges of policing speech in the age of social media. The speed and scale of online communication means that hate speech can spread quickly and reach a large audience. However, it is not always clear where the line should be drawn between free speech and hate speech, and how to enforce these distinctions in practice. As social media continues to play an increasingly central role in public discourse, it is likely that we will see more cases like this in the future, and debates around freedom of speech and hate speech will continue to be a key issue.

In short, social media provides oxygen for the fire when it comes to extremist views and opinions. Even sending a WhatsApp with extreme views can be dangerous. All of this leads to one question: what does my freedom of speech and views on politics, religion and race have to do with my job? Well, nothing as long as you keep them to yourself. When you share your peculiar opinion on any social media platform, you are engaging with the world - and this then does affect your workplace, especially if this opinion is not popular. It can even get you into trouble with authorities. Don't assume the freedom of speech argument is going to save you.

What is posted online remains accessible indefinitely:

The internet is often referred to as a vast and endless ocean of information. It is a place where we can access data, connect with people from all over the world, and share our thoughts and experiences. However, the internet is not just a place where we can find information, but it is also a vast and ever-growing memory bank that records everything that we do online.

When we post something on the internet, it becomes a part of this collective memory that is the internet. Even if we delete a post or a photo, it is never really gone. In fact, there are countless examples of how the internet has a long memory and how seemingly deleted information can resurface at any time.

One of the most obvious examples of the internet's memory is the Wayback Machine. The Wayback Machine is an online archive of the internet that allows users to access archived versions of websites. It was first launched in 1996 and has since been collecting data from websites all over the world. Today, the Wayback Machine has over 900 billion web pages in its archive. This means that even if a website is taken down, it can still be accessed through the Wayback Machine.

Another example of the internet's memory is the Streisand Effect. The Streisand Effect is a phenomenon where an attempt to hide, remove, or censor information has the unintended consequence of publicising the information more widely. The term was coined after Barbra Streisand tried to suppress photographs of her house in Malibu, California, which had been taken as part of a survey of the coastline. However, her attempts to suppress the photographs only drew more attention to them, and they ended up being seen by many more people than they would have been otherwise. We'll come back to this particular example a little later in the book - but this is a very important mental note to make, the internet does not always do what you ask of it.

Social media platforms are also a prime example of the internet's memory. When we post something on a social media platform, it becomes a part of our online identity. Even if we delete a post or a photo, it can still be accessed by others who have saved it or taken a screenshot.

Moreover, social media companies themselves also store our data, even after we delete it from our profiles. They keep records of our posts, our likes, and our interactions with other users. This information is used to build a profile of us, which is then used to serve us targeted ads. Even if we delete our social media profiles, the data that we have shared is still stored on the company's servers. What we post, write or share on social media will always exist in some form, much like a ship that sunk to the bottom of the ocean might not be visible but is there nevertheless.

The internet's memory also has implications for our privacy and security. Our personal information, such as our names, addresses, and phone numbers, can be found online through a simple Google search. This information can be used by malicious actors for identity theft, fraud, and other nefarious purposes. It is important to be vigilant about our online privacy and take steps to protect our personal information.

In conclusion, the internet's memory is vast and ever-growing. Everything that we do online becomes a part of this collective memory, and even if we delete something, it can still be accessed or can resurface at any time. It is important to be mindful of what we post online and take steps to protect our personal information. As technology continues to advance, the internet's memory will only become more powerful, and we must be prepared to navigate this complex digital landscape. All of this might scare you - and that is exactly what I intended when I wrote this. This does not mean that I believe you should never post on any social media site, my intention is simply that you post intentionally, think about what you post and are prepared to be married to it.

You are not (in)visible:

Have you posted something on a forum believing that you are posting it anonymously? And why did you choose to post it anonymously? Anonymity allows people to express themselves without fear of repercussions, which has led to the creation of various online communities that share similar interests, beliefs, and ideologies. However, despite the illusion of anonymity, the truth is that no one is truly anonymous on the internet.

Anonymity on the internet refers to the ability to participate in online activities, such as posting comments, sharing content, or sending messages without revealing your real identity. This can be achieved through the use of pseudonyms or anonymous accounts, which do not disclose any personal information about the user. Anonymity has many advantages, such as protecting people from harassment, allowing them to discuss sensitive topics without fear of retribution, and enabling them to share their opinions and ideas without judgement.

However, the reality is that anonymity on the internet is not as secure as it may seem. Firstly, websites and social media platforms collect vast amounts of data about their users, including IP addresses, search histories, and device information. This data can be used to identify users, even if they are using a pseudonym. For example, if someone logs into their anonymous social media account from their home computer, their IP address can be used to trace their physical location.

Secondly, even if someone uses a VPN or Tor to hide their IP address, they are still not completely anonymous. Websites and social media platforms can use various techniques to identify users, such as tracking their online behaviour, analysing their writing style, or identifying their device characteristics. These techniques are known as "digital fingerprinting" and can be used to identify users even if they are using a pseudonym and a VPN.

Thirdly, even if someone manages to remain completely anonymous on the internet, they are still vulnerable to hacking and cyber-attacks. Cybercriminals can use various techniques, such as phishing or social engineering, to trick people into revealing their personal information, such as their name, address, or phone number. Once this information is obtained, the user's anonymity is compromised, and they can be subjected to harassment, doxing, or identity theft.

The point I am trying to make is that you are not anonymous. And there are various ways that you can be revealed as the person behind a post, video or comment. Do not think that posting something from a pseudonym can protect you, because it is simply not true. However, you conduct yourself on social platforms, make sure it is in line with what you are comfortable sharing in your own name, even when using an anonymous account.

The virtual world is often seen as a place of escapism, where people can create a perfect version of themselves and live out their version of a fairy-tale. However, the truth is that the virtual world is not a fantasy, it is in fact real life. The Paul Chambers trial, also known as the "Twitter joke trial," is a perfect example of how the virtual world can have real-world consequences.

The Paul Chambers trial took place in 2010 and involved a man who was frustrated with the closure of an airport due to snow. He tweeted a joke that read, "Crap! Robin Hood airport is closed. You've got a week and a bit to get your shit together otherwise I'm blowing the airport sky high!" The tweet was meant as a harmless joke, but it was taken seriously by the authorities who arrested and charged Chambers with sending a "threatening message."

The case was widely criticised by many people who saw it as an overreaction by the authorities. Chambers was supported by a number of high-profile individuals, including Stephen Fry and Al Murray, who saw the case as an attack on freedom of speech. Despite this, Chambers was found guilty and fined £385, as well as being ordered to pay £600 in costs.

The Paul Chambers trial highlights the fact that the virtual world is not a separate entity from the real world. The tweet that Chambers sent may have been made in the virtual world, but the consequences were very real. He was arrested, charged, and found guilty of a crime, all because of a joke he made on Twitter.

This case also raises important questions about freedom of speech in the virtual world. And although we have covered this - here is another example of how that argument went very wrong for this individual. While many people view the virtual world as a place where they can express themselves freely, the reality is that there are often consequences for what is said online. In some cases, such as the Paul Chambers trial, these consequences can be very serious. The laws that apply in the real world also apply online, and people need to be aware of this. It is important to remember that the virtual world is not a separate entity from the real world. What is said and done online can have very real consequences.

The Paul Chambers trial also highlights the fact that the virtual world can be used as evidence in legal cases. In this case, Chambers' tweet was used as evidence against him in court. This shows that what is said and done in the virtual world can be used against individuals in the real world. It is important for people to be aware of this and to think carefully about what they post online. The virtual world is not a separate entity from the real world, and people need to remember this when they are online.

Context, tone, and audience:

In today's digital age, posting content online has become an essential part of our daily lives. From social media platforms to online forums and blogs, the internet offers various platforms for people to express their views and opinions. However, while posting online, it is crucial to consider the three essential factors: where, how, and to whom. These three factors play a vital role in ensuring that the message you are conveying reaches the right audience and has the desired impact. In this article, we will explore the significance of these three factors and how to make the most out of them.

Where to Post Online:

Choosing the right platform to post your content online is crucial. There are numerous social media platforms, online forums, blogs, and websites available, each catering to different audiences. For instance, if you are looking to connect with friends and family, social media platforms like Facebook, Twitter, and Instagram are ideal. However, if you are looking to engage with a broader audience or share your expertise on a specific topic, platforms like LinkedIn or Medium are better suited.

Another important consideration when choosing where to post online is the type of content you are sharing. For example, if you are sharing visual content like photos or videos, platforms like Instagram, TikTok, or YouTube are better suited. On the other hand, if you are sharing more text-heavy content like articles or blog posts, platforms like Medium or WordPress are more appropriate.

How to Post Online:

The way you post your content online is also essential. Whether it's the language you use, the format of your post, or the tone of your message, how you present your content online can have a significant impact on how it is received. Here are a few tips on how to post online effectively:

1. Be clear and concise: Make sure your message is clear and concise, avoiding any unnecessary jargon or complex language.
2. Use visuals: Visual content like images or videos can be more engaging and increase the likelihood of your post being shared.
3. Use appropriate formatting: Break up long blocks of text into smaller paragraphs, use headings and subheadings, and use bullet points to make your content more readable.

4. Be consistent: Consistency is key when it comes to posting online. Stick to a regular schedule, and make sure your posts are aligned with your brand or message.

To Whom to Post Online:

Understanding your audience is essential when posting online. Knowing who you are addressing and what their interests and needs are can help you tailor your message to be more effective. Here are a few tips on how to post online to the right audience:

1. Know your target audience: Research your target audience to understand their interests, preferences, and needs.
2. Use relevant hashtags: Using relevant hashtags can help your content reach a broader audience who are interested in similar topics.
3. Engage with your audience: Respond to comments and messages, and engage with your audience to build a relationship and establish credibility.
4. Personalise your message: Tailor your message to your audience's interests and needs, making it more relevant and engaging.

In conclusion, where, how, and to whom you post online are crucial considerations when it comes to making the most out of your online presence. By carefully selecting the right platform, presenting your content effectively, and targeting the right audience, you can ensure that your message reaches the right people and has the desired impact. With these tips, you can make your online presence a success and connect with your audience in a more meaningful way.

When posting online, context and tone are two critical aspects to consider to ensure that your message is received as intended. The context of your message refers to the circumstances or background surrounding the message, including the audience, the platform, and the purpose of your post. The tone, on the other hand, refers to the emotional or personal expression conveyed in your message, including the language, style, and attitude you adopt. Here's why context and tone are important when posting online:

Context:

Posting online requires a thorough understanding of the platform and audience you are addressing. Different platforms cater to different audiences and purposes, and the tone and language you use can vary widely depending on the context. For instance, if you are posting on a professional platform like LinkedIn, you may want to adopt a more formal tone and language, while a platform like Twitter may allow for a more casual or conversational tone. Understanding the context of your message can help you tailor your message to be more effective, relevant, and engaging to your audience.

Tone:

The tone of your message can significantly impact how it is received by your audience. Your tone can influence the emotions, attitudes, and perceptions of your audience, and can determine whether your message is perceived as positive, neutral, or negative. The language and style you use can also impact your tone, and it's essential to strike a balance between being informative, persuasive, and respectful. A negative or aggressive tone can turn off your audience, while a positive and engaging tone can help you build a strong relationship with your audience.

In conclusion, context and tone are two essential factors to consider when posting online. By understanding the context of your message and tailoring your tone to be more effective, you can ensure that your message is received as intended and has the desired impact. Posting online requires careful consideration and attention to detail, and by keeping context and tone in mind, you can make the most out of your online presence and engage with your audience in a meaningful way.

The workplace in the era of technology:

In today's digital age, social media has become an integral part of our lives, and it has a significant impact on the job market. Employers often use social media to research potential employees, and it has become a common practice in the recruitment process. However, what most employees fail to realise is that their online activity is being monitored by their bosses, and it can be used to fire them.

One of the ways that employers monitor their employees' online activity is through social media screening. This is a process where employers review a potential candidate's social media profiles to assess their character, values, and behaviour. Social media screening is often used to evaluate the suitability of a candidate for a particular role, and it can be a deciding factor in the hiring process.

Once you're employed, your boss will still monitor your social media activity to ensure that you are adhering to the company's values and standards. For instance, if an employee shares sensitive company information on social media, it could harm the company's reputation, and the employer might consider it as a breach of contract, leading to termination.

Another reason why employers monitor their employees' social media activity is to ensure that they are not engaging in any activity that could harm the company's reputation. For example, if an employee posts controversial content that is related to the company, it could damage the company's image, leading to loss of customers and revenue. Therefore, employers monitor their employees' online activity to prevent any negative impact on the company's image and brand.

Moreover, social media can be used as evidence to support a decision to fire an employee. If an employee posts content that is discriminatory, defamatory, or violates the company's policies, the employer can use it as evidence to support their decision to terminate the employee's contract. In such cases, the employer has the legal right to terminate the employee's contract based on the content they posted on social media.

Another way social media can be used to fire an employee is if the employee is spending too much time on social media during work hours. Employers expect their employees to be productive during working hours, and if an employee spends too much time on social media, it can affect their productivity, leading to a loss in revenue for the company. Therefore, employers monitor their employees' internet activity to ensure that they are not wasting company time on social media.

In conclusion, social media has become an essential aspect of our lives, and it has a significant impact on the job market. Employers use social media to research potential candidates and monitor their employees' online activity to ensure that they are adhering to the company's values and standards. Social media can be used as evidence to support a decision to fire an employee, especially if the content they post is discriminatory, defamatory, or violates the company's policies. Therefore, it is crucial for employees to be mindful of their online activity and ensure that they are not posting content that could harm the company's reputation or violate the company's policies.

In addition to the impact of social media on employment, it can also play a crucial role in larger company law cases. Social media can be used as evidence in cases related to intellectual property, corporate fraud, and other legal disputes.

For instance, social media can be used to prove that a company or individual has violated intellectual property rights. If a company or individual is using someone else's intellectual property without permission, they can be sued for copyright infringement. Social media can be used as evidence to show that the company or individual was using the copyrighted material without permission.

Social media can also be used in corporate fraud cases. If a company is engaging in fraudulent activities such as embezzlement or money laundering, social media can be used to prove that the company was aware of the illegal activity. Employees who have knowledge of the fraud can use social media to provide evidence to support their claims.

Moreover, social media can be used in cases related to discrimination and harassment. If an employee experiences discrimination or harassment in the workplace, they can use social media to provide evidence to support their claims. For example, if an employee is being harassed by their boss, they can provide screenshots of the harassing messages to support their claim.

In conclusion, social media can be a valuable tool in larger company law cases. It can be used as evidence to prove copyright infringement, corporate fraud, and discrimination and harassment. Therefore, it is important for companies to have clear social media policies and for employees to be mindful of their online activity to avoid any legal disputes.

You've been tagged:

Social media has become an integral part of our lives. It enables us to connect with people from all over the world, share our thoughts and experiences, and keep up-to-date with the latest news and trends. However, social media can also have a negative impact on our lives, especially when it comes to our careers. In this essay, I will discuss how being tagged on social media can affect your next job application.

When you are tagged on social media, it means that someone has mentioned you or posted something about you. This could be a photo, a video, or even a comment. While being tagged can be flattering, it can also be damaging, especially if the content is inappropriate or unprofessional.

Employers nowadays often check the social media profiles of their potential employees before hiring them. They do this to get a better sense of who the person is, and whether they would be a good fit for the company. If an employer comes across something negative about you on social media, it can affect your chances of getting hired.

For example, if you are tagged in a photo that shows you partying or drinking excessively, it can create the impression that you are not serious about your work, or that you have a problem with alcohol. This could be enough to put off an employer, especially if the company has strict policies around alcohol use.

Similarly, if you are tagged in a post that contains inappropriate or offensive content, it could reflect badly on you, and make you appear unprofessional. Even if you didn't post the content yourself, being associated with it can be damaging.

To avoid this kind of situation, it's important to be mindful of what you post on social media, and who you allow to tag you. You can also adjust your privacy settings to limit who can see your posts and photos.

Another way to mitigate the risk of being tagged in something negative is to monitor your social media profiles regularly. This way, you can quickly remove any content that might be damaging to your reputation.

In conclusion, being tagged on social media can affect your next job application in a negative way, especially if the content is inappropriate or unprofessional. To avoid this, it's important to be mindful of what you post on social media, and who you allow to tag you. You should also monitor your social media profiles regularly, and adjust your privacy settings to limit who can see your posts and photos. By doing these things, you can help protect your professional reputation and improve your chances of getting hired.

Potential repercussions of a social media mistake:

There's a great deal of uncertainty and controversy over the exact balance of employee, employer social media interconnections.

The case law of Mr Law vs Game is a key example of this, and it highlights the disciplinary consequences of social media slip-ups. In the case of Mr Law vs Game, the claimant was employed by Game as a store manager. He had been employed for 30 years and had a good disciplinary record.

However, he was dismissed after posting a message on his personal Facebook page, which the employer considered to be offensive. The post in question read: "I've been at work all day and all I've seen is a bunch of lazy, entitled, and stupid people." When the post was discovered, the employer launched an investigation and concluded that it was an offensive statement. Mr. Law was subsequently dismissed. Mr. Law took the case to the Employment Tribunal, arguing that his dismissal was unfair and that the post was not in breach of any company policies.

The tribunal agreed with him, noting that the post was on his personal Facebook page and that it did not mention any names or identify any individuals. The tribunal also noted that the post was not likely to damage the employer's reputation or undermine their relationship with customers. As a result, the tribunal ruled that the dismissal was unfair and that Mr. Law should be reinstated.

The case of Mr Law vs Game demonstrates the power of social media and the need for employers to be aware of the potential implications of employees' posts. The case also highlights the importance of having clear policies in place regarding the use of social media and the need for employers to be aware of the disciplinary consequences of any slip-ups. It is important for employers to remember that they do not have full control over what their employees post on social media. While employers can take steps to prevent or discourage inappropriate posts, they must be aware that any disciplinary action taken in response to an employee's post must be proportionate and reasonable.

Employers must also ensure that any disciplinary action taken is in line with the company's policies and procedures, and must be aware of the risk of a successful unfair dismissal claim if they fail to do so. However, this case also has an adverse effect in that many companies have a social media policy now and therefore will have grounds for dismissal or disciplinary action in case of an offensive social media post by an employee.

This book is definitely not an etiquette guide, in saying that I will dish out one sentence of advice my mother taught me well. If you cannot say anything nice, keep your mouth shut.

It's over:

Terminating an employment relationship is a difficult decision for both the employer and the employee. In today's digital age, it is important to consider how to navigate termination of the employment relationship, a digital parting of ways on social media and online. In order to ensure a respectful and professional digital parting of ways, employers and employees should consider the following tips.

1. Communicate Openly & Respectfully: The first tip when it comes to navigating the digital parting of ways is to communicate openly and respectfully. This means being transparent and honest with each other about the reasons for the termination, as well as ensuring that each party understands the terms of the termination. It is also important to remain professional and courteous when communicating online, even if the situation is difficult or emotional.

2. Update Social Media Profiles: Once the termination is finalised, it is important for both the employer and the employee to update their social media profiles. For the employer, this may include removing the employee from company accounts and updating job titles and descriptions. For the employee, this could mean changing the job title and company name on their personal profile, so that it is clear they are no longer affiliated with the company.

3. Resolve Any Outstanding Issues: Before the digital parting of ways, it is important for both parties to resolve any outstanding issues, such as the terms of the employee's severance package or the return of company property. This is a critical step in order to ensure that both parties are in agreement and to avoid any potential legal issues down the road.

4. Review & Remove Any Negative Content: It is also important to review and remove any negative content that may be posted on social media or online about the former employee or employer. This includes any posts, comments, or reviews that may be perceived as negative or inappropriate. This can help to ensure that the digital parting of ways is respected and professional.

5. Monitor & Maintain the Relationship: Finally, it is important to monitor and maintain the relationship between the employer and the former employee even after the digital parting of ways. This may include staying in contact with each other, as well as keeping an eye on any potential job opportunities for the former employee.

This can help to ensure that the digital parting of ways remains respectful and professional. Navigating the digital parting of ways can be challenging for both employers and employees. By following these tips, employers and employees can ensure that the termination of their employment relationship is respectful and professional. This can help to ensure a positive experience for both parties and can help to maintain the relationship even after the digital parting of ways.

Managing social media platforms:

I am no social media expert and will not be able to help you gain followers or get sponsors for your page, however there are certain helpful rules to help you keep in the clear when posting on behalf of your company on a public profile. This may be on the company profile or on your own profile tagging your company to promote something specific.

1. Respect your audience - Always respond to messages, questions, and comments in a timely and professional manner.

2. Know the rules - Familiarise yourself with the platform's policies and stay current on any relevant changes.

3. Stay on brand - Maintain a consistent tone and voice in all of your social media posts.

4. Be positive - Avoid posting anything negative about your company, customers, or competitors.

5. Follow the law - Do not post anything that might be considered defamatory or libellous.

6. Protect confidential information - Keep confidential or proprietary information from being shared on social media.

7. Monitor the conversation - Pay attention to what other users are saying about your company, its products and services, and its competitors.

8. Respect copyright - Do not repost or share content without permission.

9. Be transparent - Let followers know when you are posting sponsored content.

10. Track your progress - Monitor and evaluate your social media performance to ensure your efforts are yielding the desired results.

The Streisand effect:

The Streisand effect has come up previously in this book, it's a phenomenon that occurs when an attempt to censor or suppress information results in the unintended consequence of drawing more attention to it. The term was coined in 2003 when American singer/actress Barbra Streisand attempted to sue a photographer for publishing an aerial photo of her Malibu home, and inadvertently brought more attention to the photo than it would have received otherwise. Today, the Streisand Effect has become a major issue in the age of digital media and social networks, playing out in real time with high profile cases. The most recent example is the Giggs vs Twitter case, where British rapper Giggs attempted to use the courts to force Twitter to reveal the identity of a user who had posted a disparaging tweet about him.

By taking legal action, Giggs drew more attention to the tweet, ultimately leading to the Streisand Effect. The Giggs vs Twitter case is a prime example of how the Streisand Effect can work in the digital world. Before Giggs took legal action, the tweet had been seen by only a handful of people. But after Giggs' case went public, the tweet began to spread rapidly, and soon it was being shared and discussed by hundreds of thousands of people. As a result, the tweet was seen by far more people than it would have been had Giggs simply ignored it.

The Streisand Effect is not only applicable to cases involving celebrities, however. Businesses, organisations and even ordinary people have become victims of the Streisand Effect when they attempt to censor or suppress information. For example, a company might try to remove negative reviews from their website, only to find that the reviews have been reposted and shared by thousands of people. The Streisand Effect has become increasingly relevant in the age of social media, where information can spread quickly and reach a large audience. As such, it's important to consider the potential consequences of attempting to censor or suppress information before taking action. The Giggs vs Twitter case is a prime example of how attempting to censor information can lead to the unintended consequence of drawing more attention to it.

It's important to note that once a social media post, whether it be tweet or WhatsApp has been sent, you have little to no control over who took a screenshot, forwarded or reposted it even if you delete it later on, this might have already been shared seconds after you have sent it.

How to stay out of trouble:

The internet is an incredible resource that allows us to access information, stay connected with friends, and engage with the world in ways we never could before. However, it is also a place full of potential pitfalls and dangers. It is important to understand the ways that people can get into trouble online in order to stay safe and secure. Here are a few "golden rules" for staying out of trouble online.

1. Be aware of the people you interact with: It is extremely important to be aware of the people you interact with online. There are many people who may try to take advantage of you or manipulate you into doing something you do not want to do. Be sure to take the time to learn about the people you are interacting with, and make sure they are who they say they are. Do not trust anyone you meet online, and always be wary of any requests that seem suspicious.

2. Do not share personal information: It is important to remember that anything you post online can be seen by anyone. It is best to avoid sharing personal information such as your address, phone number, or credit card information. Even if you think you are only sharing this information with a trusted friend, you should still be mindful of how it could be used against you. It is best to only share this information with people you know and trust in real life.

3. Use strong passwords: As you use more and more websites, it is important to create strong passwords for each one. Weak passwords are easy to guess, and can be used to gain access to your accounts. Your passwords should be long, complex, and unique. You should also avoid using the same password for multiple accounts.

4. Be mindful of what you post: Be sure to think twice before you post anything online. Even if you are just joking around, it is important to be aware of the fact that people may take what you say seriously. Anything you post can be seen by a large number of people, so it is important to make sure it is something you are comfortable with.

5. Be aware of scams: There are a variety of scams out there, and it is important to be aware of them. Be suspicious of any emails or messages that seem too good to be true, or requests money or personal information. If you are ever unsure about something, it is best to research it before you take any action.

6. Use caution when downloading files: Be sure to only download files from reputable sources. If you are downloading something from the internet, make sure it is from a trusted and secure website. Do not download anything from websites that are unfamiliar to you, as it could contain malicious software.

7. Keep your computer updated: It is important to keep your computer and software up to date. This will help ensure that your system is secure, and will help protect you from any malicious software.

8. Monitor your child's online activity: If you have children, it is important to monitor their online activity. Make sure they know what is appropriate to post and share online, and ensure that they are aware of the potential dangers of the internet. Following these "golden rules" will help you stay safe and secure while online. It is important to be aware of the potential risks associated with the internet. If you ever have any questions or concerns, it is best to talk to a professional who can help you navigate the online world.

If you or your company need further help in educating employees or those around you, or need content of any sort please contact me via my social media profile on Instagram @thecontent_studio.

I write personalised & ready to use content for a variety of companies whether it be website content writing, profile and tender writing or educational modules.

25

www.ingramcontent.com/pod-product-compliance
Lightning Source LLC
Chambersburg PA
CBHW071131220526
45467CB00004B/2128